SCRATCH
CODE CHALLENGE

Scratch Code
TRANSPORTATION

Max
Wainewright

I0809313

CRABTREE
PUBLISHING COMPANY
WWW.CRABTREEBOOKS.COM

CRABTREE
PUBLISHING COMPANY
WWW.CRABTREEBOOKS.COM

Author: Max Wainewright

Editorial director: Kathy Middleton

Editors: Elise Short, Crystal Sikkens

Proofreader: Melissa Boyce

Design: Peter Scoulding

Cover design: Peter Scoulding

Illustrations: John Haslam

Prepress technician: Margaret Amy Salter

Print coordinator: Katherine Berti

Every attempt has been made to clear copyright. Should there be any inadvertent omission please apply to the publisher for rectification.

Picture credits:
Shutterstock: Ryan Fletcher 6, Sergey Zaykov 10, Sanit Fuangnakhon 12, Oleksiy Mark 15, metamorworks 18, Zapp2Photo 23, FamVeld 24, Lenscap Photography 27, Alamy Stock Photo: SiliconValleyStock 20.

We recommend that children are supervised at all times when using the Internet. Some of the projects in this series use a computer webcam or microphone. Please make sure children are made aware that they should only allow a computer to access the webcam or microphone on specific websites that a trusted adult has told them to use. We do not recommend children use websites or microphones on any other websites other than those mentioned in this book.

The website addresses (URLs) included in this book were valid at the time of going to press. However, it is possible that contents or addresses may have changed since the publication of this book. No responsibility for any such changes can be accepted by either the author or the Publisher.

Scratch is developed by the Lifelong Kindergarten Group at the MIT Media Lab. See http://scratch.mit.edu.

Images and illustrations from Scratch included in this book have been developed by the Lifelong Kindergarten Group at the MIT Media Lab (see http://scratch.mit.edu) and made available under the Creative Commons Attribution-ShareAlike 2.0 license (https://creativecommons.org/licenses/by-sa/2.0/deed.en). The third party trademarks used in this book are the property of their respective owners, including the Scratch name and logo. The owners of these trademarks have not endorsed, authorized or sponsored this book.

Library and Archives Canada Cataloguing in Publication

Title: Scratch code transportation / Max Wainewright.
Other titles: Transportation
Names: Wainewright, Max, author.
Description: Series statement: Scratch code challenge | Includes index.
Identifiers: Canadiana (print) 20190107243 | Canadiana (ebook) 2019010726X | ISBN 9780778765424 (hardcover) | ISBN 9780778765707 (softcover) | ISBN 9781427123879 (HTML)
Subjects: LCSH: Scratch (Computer program language)—Juvenile literature. | LCSH: Transportation—Computer programs—Juvenile literature. | LCSH: Computer programming—Juvenile literature.
Classification: LCC QA76.73.S345 W35 2019 | DDC j005.13/3—dc23

Library of Congress Cataloging-in-Publication Data

Names: Wainewright, Max, author.
Title: Scratch code transportation / Max Wainewright.
Other titles: Transportation
Description: New York, New York : Crabtree Publishing, 2020. | Series: Scratch code challenge | Includes index.
Identifiers: LCCN 2019013625 (print) | LCCN 2019013981 (ebook) ISBN 9781427123879 (Electronic) | ISBN 9780778765424 (hardcover : alk. paper) | ISBN 9780778765707 (pbk. : alk. paper)
Subjects: LCSH: Scratch (Computer program language)--Juvenile literature. | Transportation--Computer programs--Juvenile literature. | Computer programming--Juvenile literature.
Classification: LCC QA76.73.S345 (ebook) | LCC QA76.73.S345 W3525 2020 (print) | DDC 005.13/3--dc23
LC record available at https://lccn.loc.gov/2019013625

Crabtree Publishing Company

www.crabtreebooks.com 1–800–387–7650

Published by Crabtree Publishing Company in 2020

Text copyright © ICT Apps, 2019
Art and design copyright © Hodder and Stoughton, 2019

All rights reserved. No part of this publication may be reproduced, stored in a retrieval system or be transmitted in any form or by any means, electronic, mechanical, photocopying, recording, or otherwise, without the prior written permission of Crabtree Publishing Company.

Printed in the U.S.A./072019/CG20190501

Published in Canada
Crabtree Publishing
616 Welland Ave.
St. Catharines, Ontario
L2M 5V6

Published in the United States
Crabtree Publishing
PMB 59051
350 Fifth Avenue, 59th Floor
New York, New York 10118

Contents

Words in *italics* appear in the glossary on page 31.

Introduction

In this book, you will learn how technology is used in some modern vehicles. You'll find out how computer technology is changing traditional forms of transportation and enabling brand new forms to be invented.

We'll spend some time looking at how the technology works in various types of transportation, as well as learning about the different parts of each *system*. We will also have a look inside the computer code that connects the components and brings things to life.

You'll use the *algorithms* and ideas that control real forms of transportation technology to create your own programs. These programs will help you understand how things work, and set you on the road to dreaming up your own ideas for the future of transportation!

There are a lot of different ways to create code. We will be using a website called Scratch to do our coding.

Let's start by looking at the important parts of the screen in Scratch:

File Menu (for logged-in users)
If you want, you can create a free account and save your work online. Check with a grown-up first. Alternatively, you can use the Load and Save options to open and save work on your computer.

Sound Library
Add sounds to your program from here.

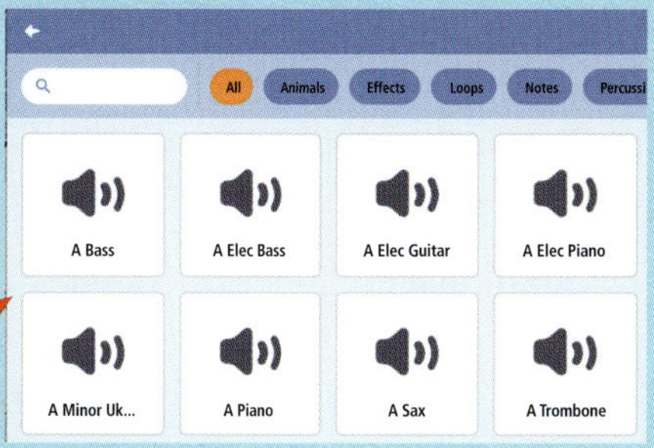

File Menu (for general users)
Choose Load and Save to open and save work on your computer.

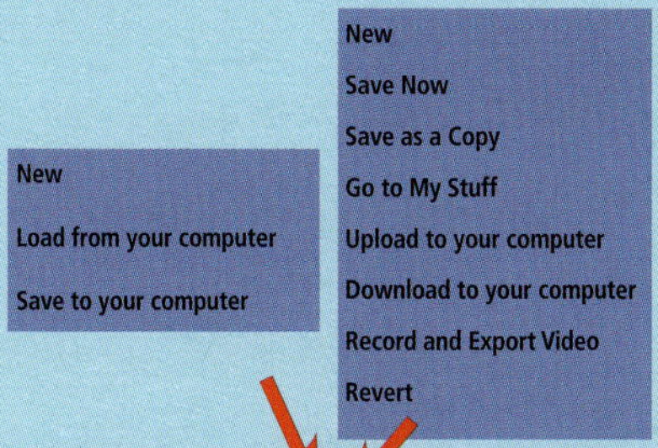

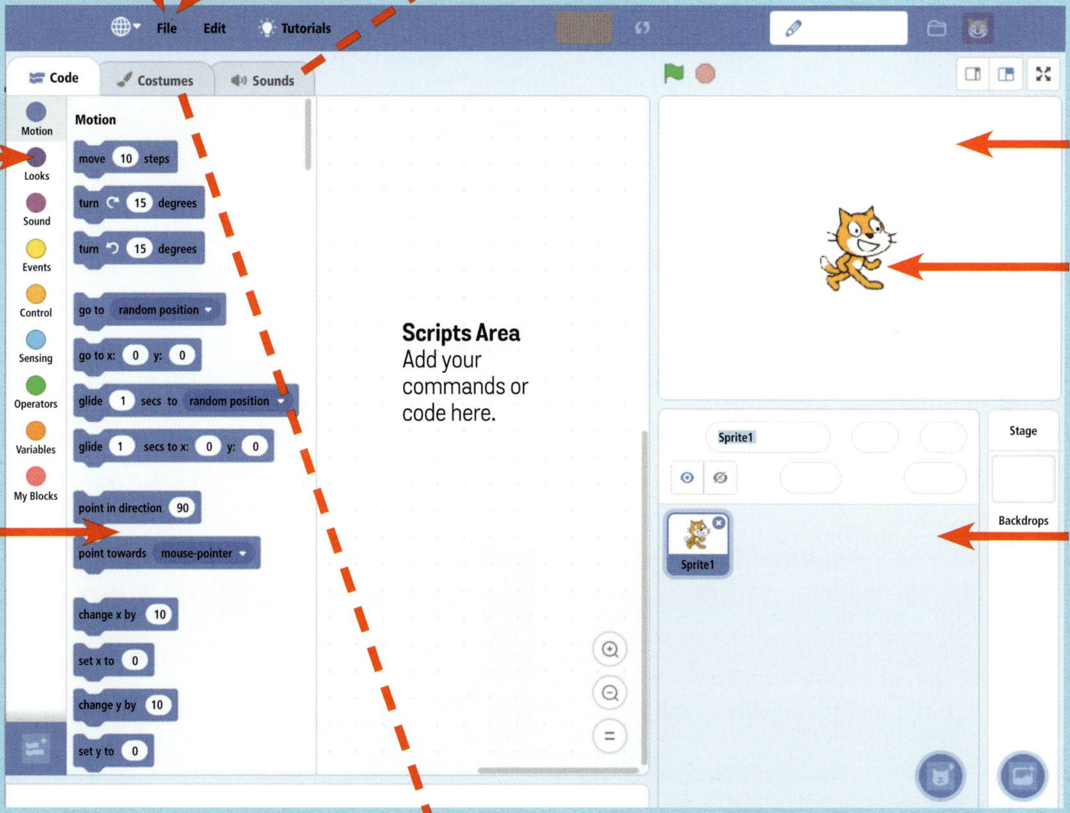

Block Categories
Choose commands from these categories.

Scripts Area
Add your commands or code here.

The Stage
Your program takes place on the *Stage*.

Sprites
Objects that move around in Scratch are called *sprites*.

List of Commands
Find the blocks you need by matching the color to the category name. For example, dark blue blocks will be found in the motion category.

Sprites Pane
Select which of your sprites you want to add code or sound to in this area.

Sprite Library
Choose ready-made sprites for your programs.

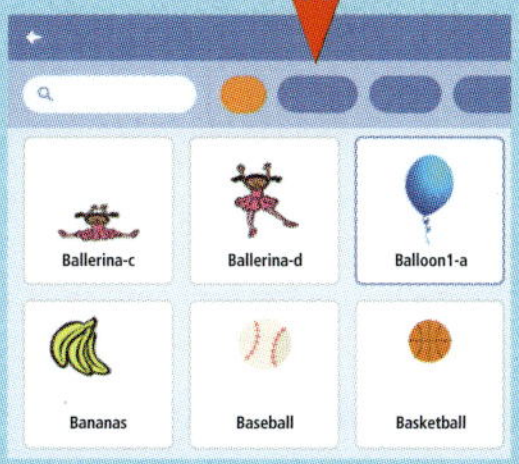

Paint Editor
This is used to draw your own sprites or backdrops.

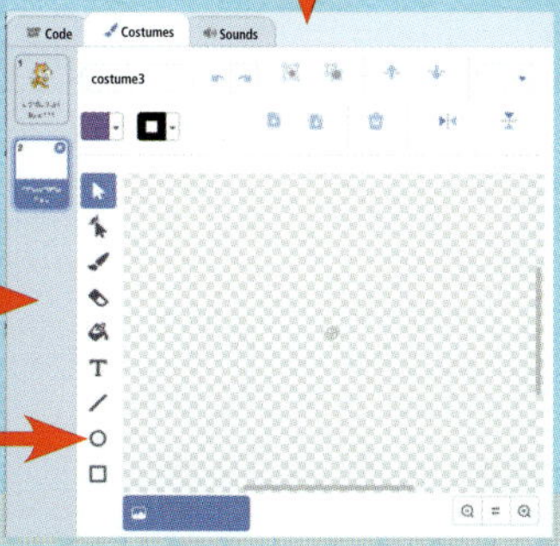

Costume Pane

Drawing Tools

Automotive Technology

The first cars were on the road over 130 years ago. These early cars were much simpler than today's vehicles.

Over time, electronics and computers started to play a bigger role in cars. Computers now control how the different components of a car are connected together. Cables and levers are being replaced by electronic switches, wires, computers, and special motors called servos. Let's build our own car with code to see how these systems work.

STEP 1 – Remove the cat

Right-click the cat sprite and click **delete**.

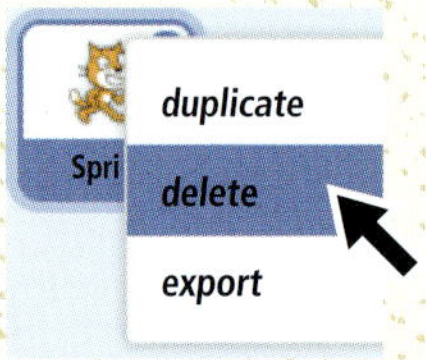

STEP 2 – Add a sprite

Hover over the **Choose a Sprite** button.

Click the **Brush** *icon*.

STEP 3 – Start drawing

Click **Convert to Bitmap**.

Select the **Rectangle** tool.

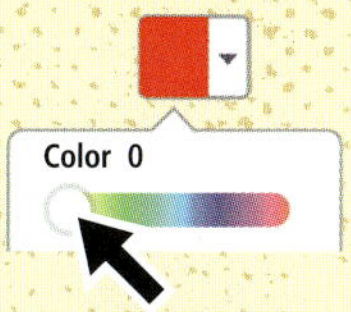

Choose a color for your car.

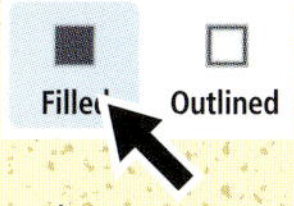

Set the rectangle to **Filled**.

STEP 4 – Draw the car

Start by drawing a rectangle. Make it about three-quarters of the width of the drawing area.

Click the **Line** tool.

Make the line thicker.

Draw the windshield.

Add a roof.

Draw the trunk...

...and the windows.

STEP 5 – Final details

Add any other details with a thinner line in a darker color.

Click the Undo tool if you make a mistake.

Round the corners off with the **Eraser**.

For help, go to: **www.maxw.com**

Hold down the shift key to make an exact circle.

STEP 6 – Draw a wheel

Hover over the **Choose a Sprite** button.

Click the **Brush** icon.

Click **Convert to Bitmap**.

Choose black.

Now click the **Ellipse** tool.

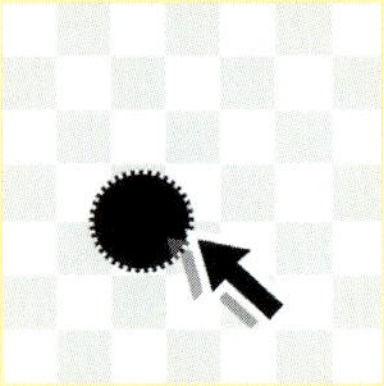

Draw the tire.

Choose gray.

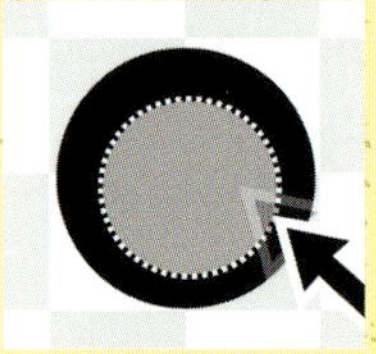

Draw the wheel inside the tire.

Drag the wheel so it's in the middle of the tire.

Use the Zoom controls to get a better view when adding small details.

Use the **Line** tool to draw dark gray spoke details on the wheel.

STEP 7 – Get coding

First, we need to make a *variable* that can store the speed of the car:

Click the **Code** tab.

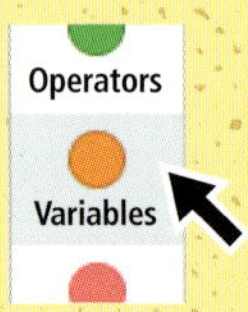

Click the **Variables** category.

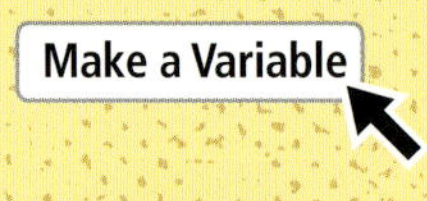

Click **Make a Variable**.

Type **speed**.

Click **OK**.

Now drag these *code blocks* into the **Scripts Area**.

Use the colors to help you find the correct group for each block.

See page 30 for help positioning blocks.

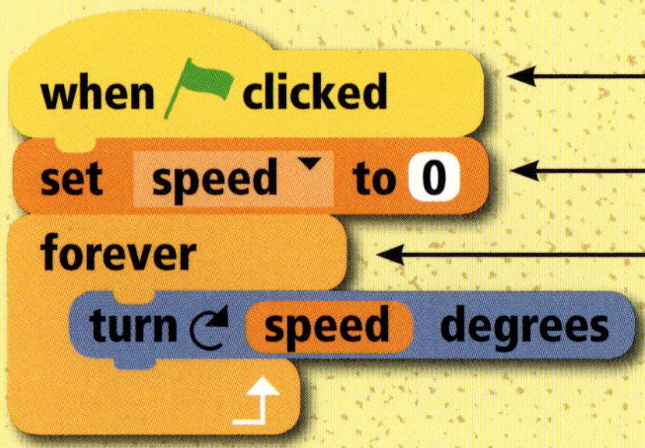

Run this code when the green flag is clicked:

Set the speed to zero.

Keep *looping* this code forever:

Rotate the wheels according to the size of the speed variable.

The Gas Pedal

How it works

When driving a car you need to control how fast it is going. You do this with the gas pedal. In traditional gas-powered cars, the throttle cable connects the pedal to the engine. Pressing the pedal harder sends more air and gas to the engine, making the engine turn faster. This then makes the wheels turn faster, and the car accelerates.

In an electric car, the pedal is connected to a computer. A *sensor* on the pedal tells the computer how far it is pressed. The computer then delivers the correct amount of energy from the battery to one or more electric motors. The motors then spin the wheels faster.

For our car, we have simplified things. Instead of a pedal, we will use a slider to change the speed.

STEP 8 – Position the front wheel

We need to move the wheel into the correct position, and set the center so it spins smoothly.

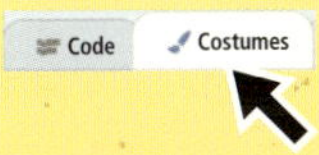

Click the **Costumes** tab.

Choose the **Select** tool.

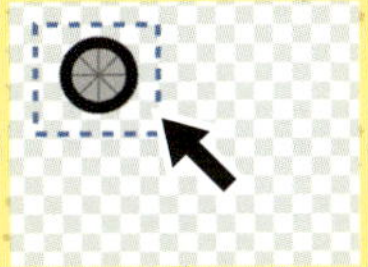

Draw around the wheel to select it.

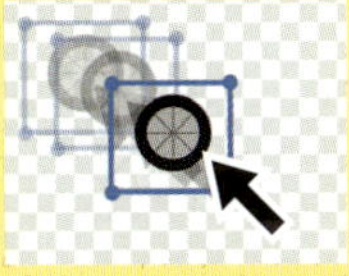

Drag the wheel to the center of the drawing area.

Now over on the Stage, drag the wheel to the front of the car.

STEP 9 – Let's go!

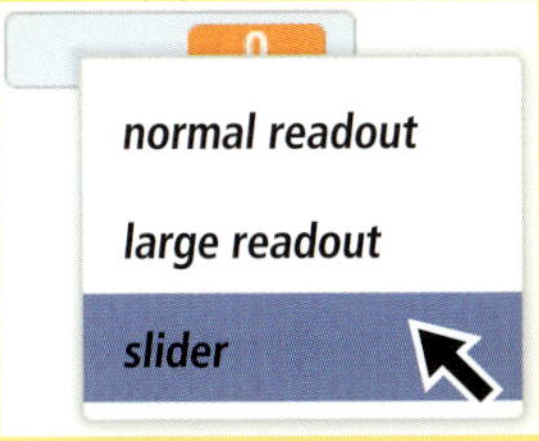

Find the speed variable in the top left corner of the screen. Hover over it and click the right mouse button. Then choose "slider."

Click the flag.

Gradually drag the slider to the right to set the speed, and watch what happens!

STEP 10 – Back wheel

Right-click the **wheel sprite**.

Click **duplicate**.

Drag the new wheel to the back.

Click the flag and move the slider to test your code again.

Let's add some other features to our car.

STEP 11 – Find sound effects

Start by finding a sound for the horn.

Click **Sprite1** (the car sprite) in the **Sprites pane**.

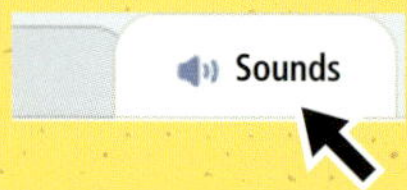

Click the **Sounds** tab.

Click the **Choose a Sound** icon.

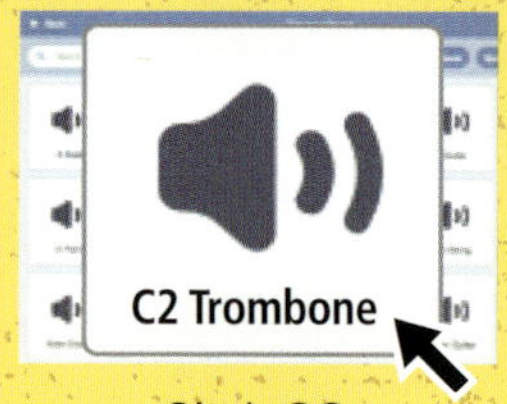

Click **C2 trombone**.

STEP 12 – Sound the horn

In most cars, we press the center of the steering wheel to sound the horn. We can sound our horn by pressing one of the keys on the keyboard.

Now click the **Code** tab and drag in this code:

```
when h key pressed          ← Run this code when the "h" key is pressed. (Choose "h" from the drop-down menu.)
start sound C2 trombone     ← Play the horn sound effect.
```

Click the flag. Now try pressing the "h" key on the keyboard.

Turn signals are used to warn other drivers that a car is about to change direction. Over time, these have evolved from a mechanical flipper to the flashing orange or red lights we have today. To make our lights flash, we will use code to hide and show them.

STEP 13 – Add turn signals

Hover over the **Choose a Sprite** button.

Click the **Brush** icon.

Click **Convert to Bitmap**.

Select the **Rectangle** tool.

Choose orange.

STEP 14 – Draw the turn signals

Draw a small rectangle.

Round the corners off with the **Eraser**.

Now drag it into place on the car.

STEP 15 – Flashing code

Click the **Code** tab and drag in this code to make it flash when the "s" key is pressed:

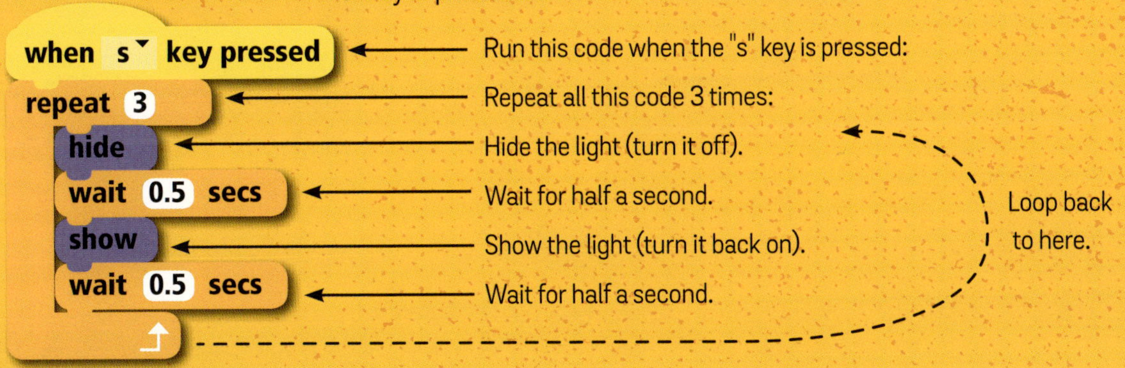

Investigate

In the flashing code, try changing the number 3 at the top of the repeat block.

What happens if you change the number of seconds in the wait command?

Code challenge

Add a second turn signal light to the back of the car.

When it gets dark, the car will need headlights. They won't need to flash. Make them turn on when you press one key, and turn off when you press another.

How about adding a radio to your car? Make it play one of the **musical loops** in the sounds tab when a key is pressed on the keyboard.

What else can you add to your car?

Drones

A drone is a flying machine similar to a helicopter—but with no pilot! Most drones are flown by remote control, with a human controlling where the drone goes.

Drones that are controlled entirely by computers are now being developed. A human tells the computer where the drone needs to go, such as an address to deliver a package, and the drone works out how to get there! Let's have a look at how they work and build our own on-screen drone with code.

STEP 1 – Remove the cat

Right-click the cat sprite and click **delete**.

STEP 2 – Add a sprite

Hover over the **Choose a Sprite** button.

Click the **Brush** icon.

STEP 3 – Draw the frame

Click **Convert to Bitmap**.

Select the **Line** tool.

Choose a color for the drone.

Make the line thicker.

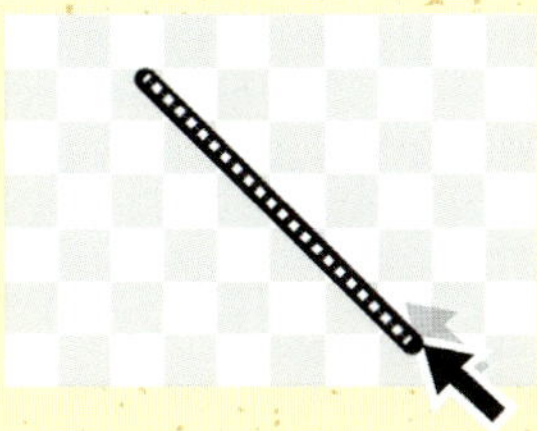

Start the frame with a line.

Add a second line.

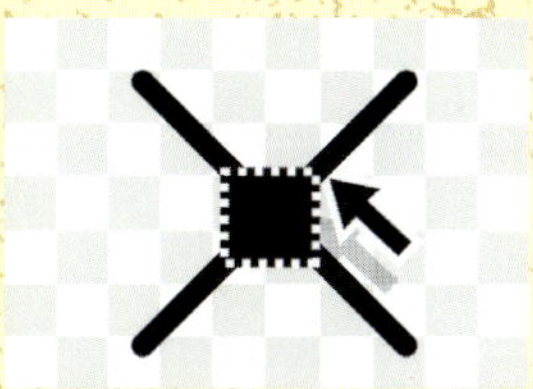

Choose **Rectangle** and select **Filled**. Complete the drone frame.

STEP 4 – Add the propeller

Hover over the **Choose a Sprite** button.

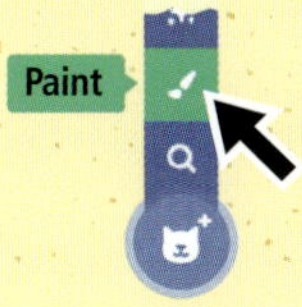

Click the **Brush** icon.

Click **Convert to Bitmap**.

Select the **Ellipse** tool.

Choose a color.

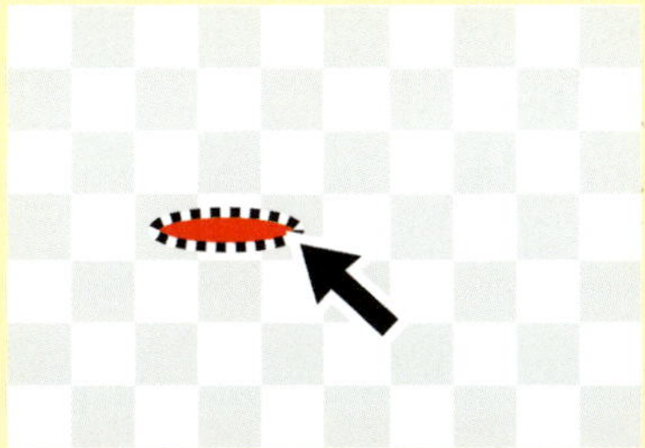

Draw a small, thin oval in the center of the drawing area.

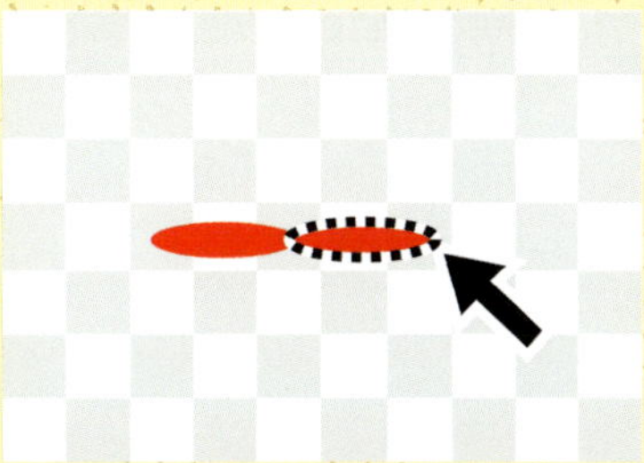

Add a second oval to complete the propeller.

STEP 5 – Position the propellor

Choose the **Select** tool.

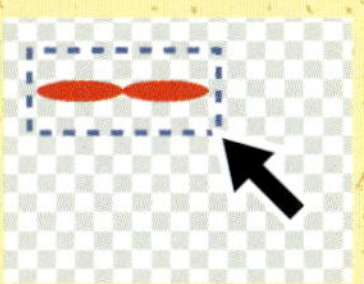

Draw around the propeller to select it.

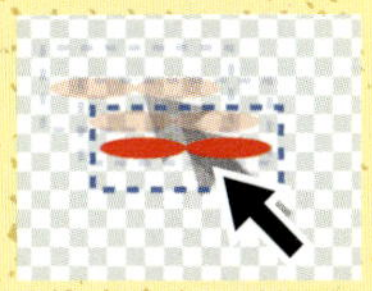

Drag it to the center of the drawing area.

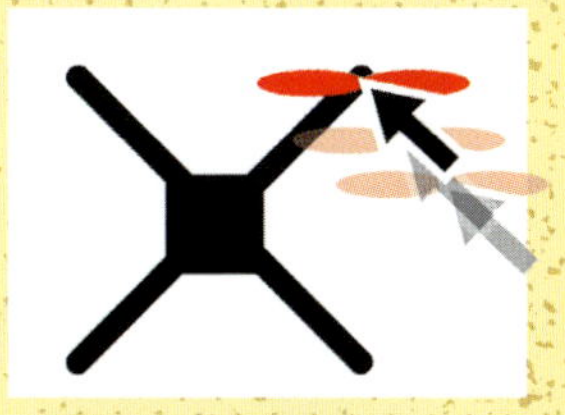

On the Stage, drag the propeller to one edge of the drone's frame.

STEP 6 – Get coding

We need a variable that can store the speed of the propeller.

Click the **Code** tab.

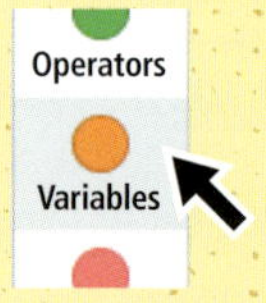

Click the **Variables** category.

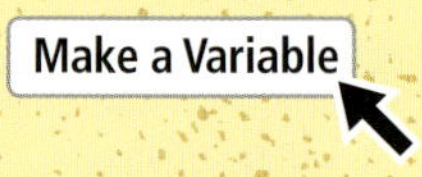

Click **Make a Variable.**

Type **speed.**

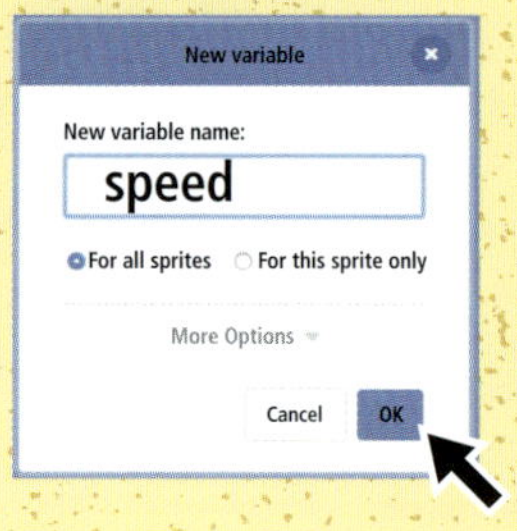

Click **OK.**

Now drag in this code.

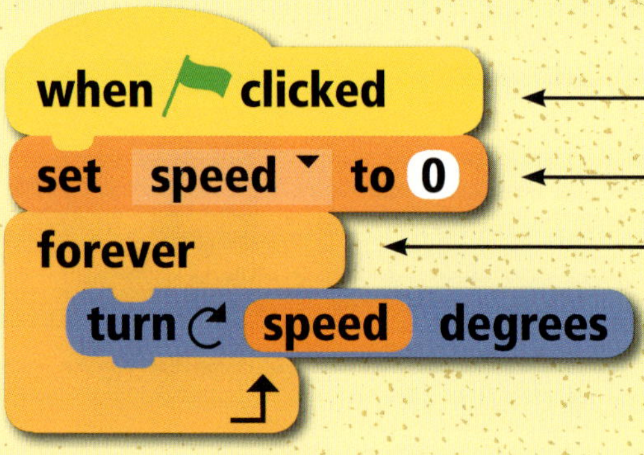

Run this code when the green flag is clicked:

Set the speed to zero.

Keep looping this code forever:

Rotate the propeller according to the value of the speed variable. (Drag in speed from the Variables group.)

STEP 7 – Take off!

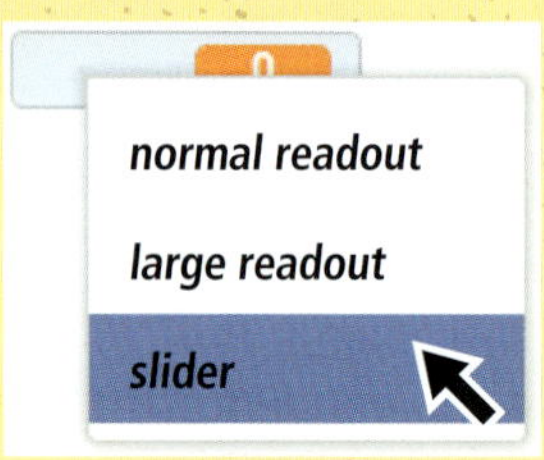

Find the speed variable in the top left corner of the Stage screen. Right-click on it, then choose **slider**.

Click the flag.

Gradually drag the slider to the right to set the speed of the propeller.

STEP 8 – More propellers

Right-click the **propeller sprite**.

Click **duplicate**.

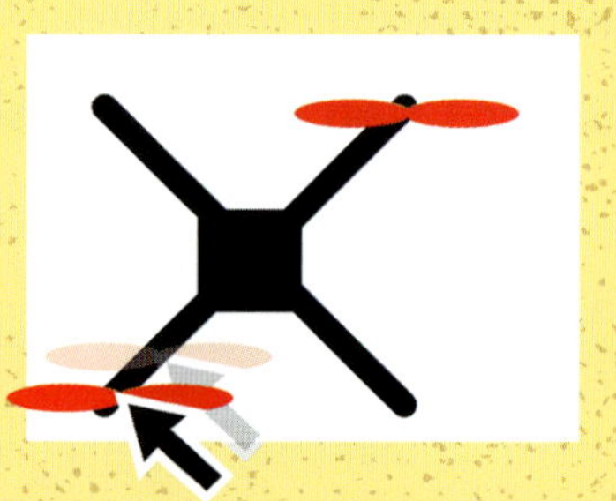

Drag the new propeller into the corner opposite the first one.

STEP 9 – Opposite direction

The other two propellers need to spin in the opposite direction to make the drone fly correctly.

Repeat step 8 to duplicate another propeller.

Remove the code block that makes it rotate, by dragging it back to the block palette.

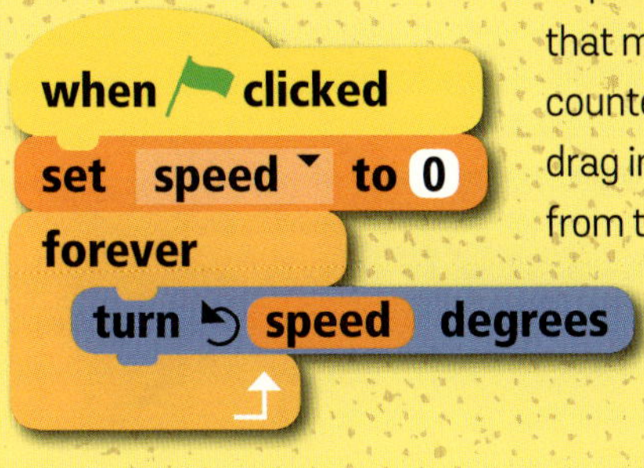

Replace it with one that makes it rotate counterclockwise and drag in the speed block from the Variables group.

Let's make the new propeller green, to differentiate it:

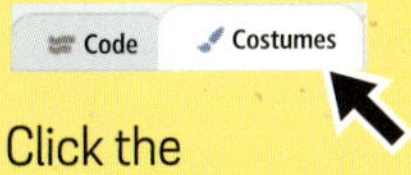

Click the **Costumes** tab.

Select green, then use the **Fill** tool to change the color.

Repeat step 8 to duplicate the final propeller.

Your drone should now look like this. Use the green flag to run your code, and the slider to control the speed of the propellers. Notice the direction each propeller rotates.

How it works

Computer
A computer controls all the different systems within the drone.

Four motors and propellers
The speed of each motor is controlled by the computer. Changing the speed of different pairs of motors makes the drone move forward, backward, or rotate. Making all the motors change speed causes the drone to go up or down.

Frame
All the components are attached to a frame or chassis.

Legs
Legs are needed to land on.

Camera
Most drones either carry a camera or some kind of load (such as a package for delivery).

GPS
A *Global Positioning System (GPS)* may be added to detect the drone's location and determine its height in relation to the ground.

Gyro
A *gyroscope (gyro)* is located inside the drone. This is used to keep the drone stable.

Destination Drone

Now that we know how drones fly, let's program a drone to make it reach a particular destination. Save your old program and start a new file in Scratch.

STEP 1 – Remove the cat

Right-click the cat sprite and click **delete**.

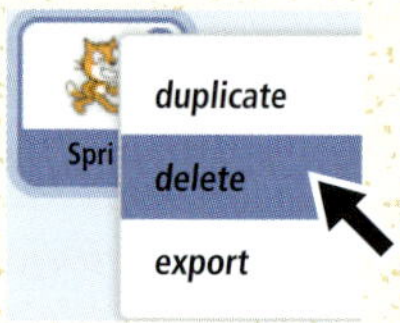

STEP 2 – Add a sprite

Hover over the **Choose a Sprite** button.

Click the **Brush** icon.

STEP 3 – Draw a drone from the side

Click **Convert to Bitmap**.

Select the **Rectangle** tool.

Choose a color for your drone.

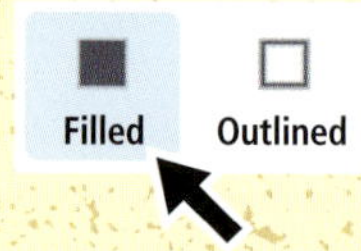

Set the rectangle to **Filled**.

Draw a thin rectangle, about half the width of the drawing area.

Click the **Ellipse** tool.

Draw a circle to house the computer and drone systems.

Add a small circle at each edge of the drone for the motors.

STEP 4 – Duplicate your costume

To make it look as though the propellors are rotating, let's create two-frame animation. We will need a second frame or "costume" for the sprite to do this. This is done by duplicating what you have just drawn.

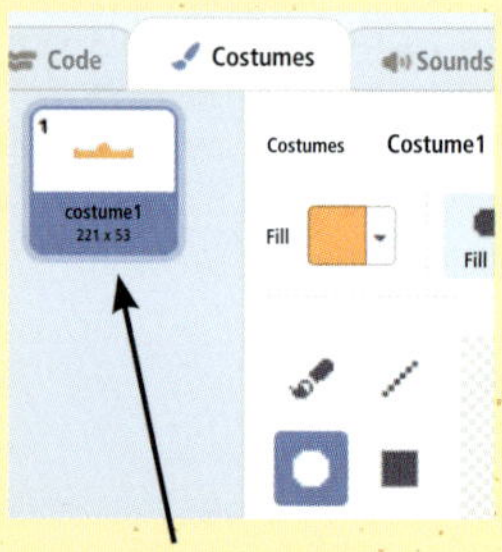

Find **costume1** in the top left of the screen, and right-click it.

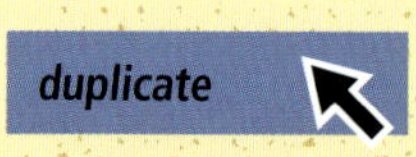

Click **duplicate**.

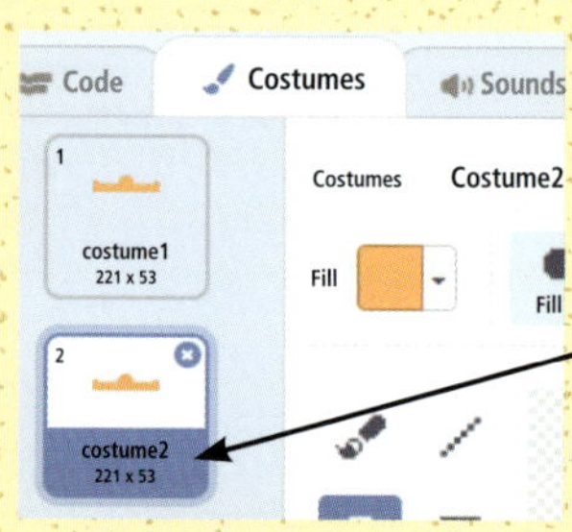

The second costume will be shown here.

For help, go to: **www.maxw.com**

STEP 5 – Costume 2

Use the **Ellipse** tool to add a green propeller blade on the left side, and a red one on the right.

STEP 6 – Costume 1

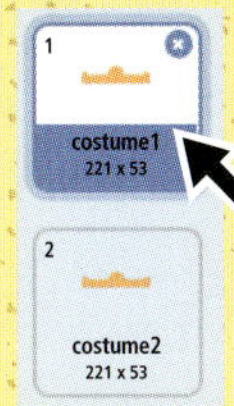

Now switch back to **costume1**.

Draw the two propellers again, but in different positions.

STEP 7 – Add code to make it fly!

Click the **Code** tab and drag in this code:

```
when [flag] clicked        ← Run this code when the green flag is clicked:
set size to (20) %         ← Shrink the drone down to 20%.
forever                    ← Keep looping this code forever:
    next costume           ← Switch costumes.
```

This section of code will keep moving between the two sprite costumes, giving the illusion that the propellers are rotating.

Now add this second section of code:

```
when [flag] clicked          ← Run this code when the green flag is clicked:
go to x: (-200) y: (-125)    ← Move to the bottom left of the screen.
repeat (200)                 ← Run this code 200 times:
    change y by (1)          ← Move the drone upward.
repeat (350)                 ← Run this code 350 times:
    change x by (1)          ← Move the drone to the right.
repeat (140)                 ← Run this code 140 times:
    change y by (-1)         ← Move the drone down.
```

This part of the code controls the path that the drone will take on its journey.

Click the flag to test your code.

Investigate

Change the values at the start of the **Repeat** blocks. What happens?

In the **change x** and **y** blocks, try swapping the 1 and −1 around. See what difference it makes.

Code challenge

Click on the **Stage** icon in the **Sprites pane**, at the bottom left of the screen. Go to the drawing area and click on **Backdrops**. Try drawing a background of a city.

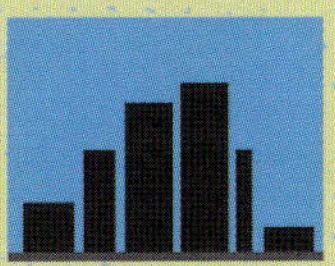

Now change the second section of code to make the drone take off from one building in the city and land on the other side. (As you move your mouse, you will see the x and y coordinates displayed on the right, below the Stage. Use the values to help you.)

Self-Driving Cars

We've already looked at how transportation technology has become more and more sophisticated. Many new cars today have computers that can help the driver. These include sensors to check if the car is too close to another, or to make sure the car is staying in its lane on a highway.

A few cars have computers that actually drive themselves for part of the trip. Not everyone thinks this is a good idea. Will self-driving cars be better drivers than humans? How does the technology work? Let's find out by coding our own self-driving car.

STEP 1 – Remove the cat

Right-click the cat sprite and click **delete**.

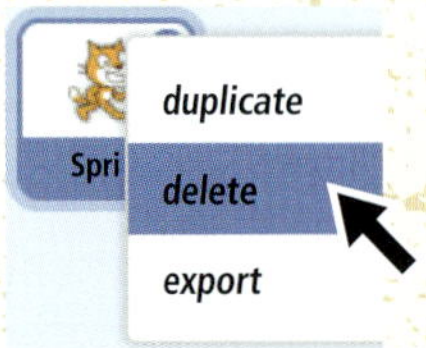

STEP 2 – Add a sprite

Hover over the **Choose a Sprite** button.

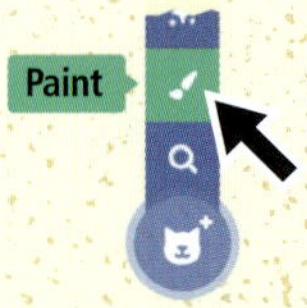

Click the **Brush** icon.

Now draw your futuristic car. Make sure you show it in plan view (drawn from above).

STEP 3 – Start drawing

Click **Convert to Bitmap**.

Select the **Rectangle** tool.

Choose a color for your car.

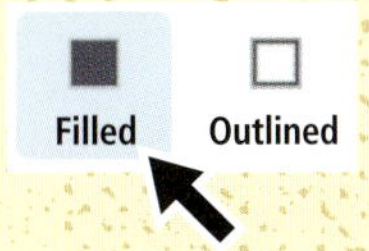

Set the rectangle to **Filled**.

STEP 4 – Draw the car

Start by drawing a rectangle. Make it about half the width of the drawing area.

Now click the **Ellipse** tool.

Draw an ellipse to make the front of the car curvy, and drag it into place.

STEP 5 – Add a windshield

Choose light gray for the glass.

Draw the windshield.

Go back to the color you chose for the body.

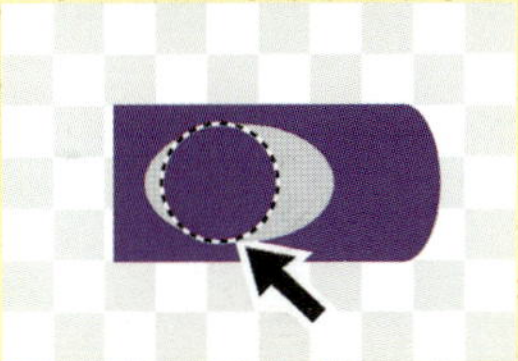

Draw the roof.

STEP 6 – Wheel arches and final details

Draw four wheel arches to make the car look more powerful and streamlined.

Maybe add some stripes with the **Line** tool!

For help, go to: **www.maxw.com**

STEP 7 – Get moving

Click the **Code** tab and drag in this code:

```
when [flag] clicked
set size to (20) %
forever
    move (2) steps
```

- Run this code when the green flag is clicked:
- Shrink the car down to 20%.
- Keep looping this code forever.
- Move the car 2 *steps* forward.

Click the flag to test the code!

STEP 8 – The background

Click on the **Stage** icon next to the **Sprites pane.**

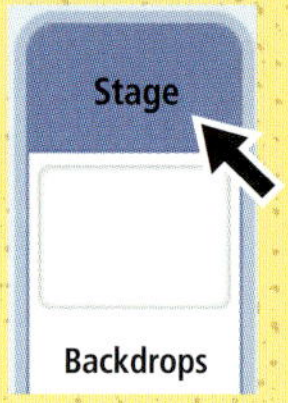

Click the **Backdrops** tab.

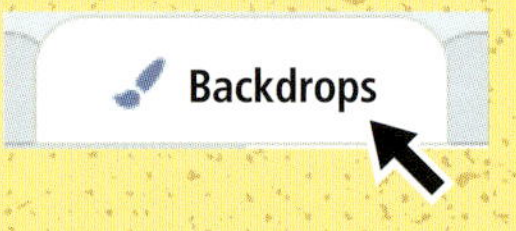

STEP 9 – Draw a road

Click **Convert to Bitmap**.

Use the **Brush** tool.

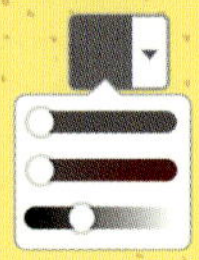

Pick dark gray.

Draw the edge of a large road. It should fill most of the space.

Now draw the inside edge of the road. Make sure there are no gaps.

Fill between the lines to make a thick gray road.

If the color leaks out, click Undo and fill up any gaps with the brush. Then try filling it again.

To keep the car on the road, we need to find a way for it to detect where the road is. Self-driving cars use sensors to do this.

Google has built a self-driving car. To detect obstacles, it has a laser scanner and radar system on top of its roof. The scanner rotates to check all around the car.

We will add a sensor on the left-hand side of the car. This will check if the car is near the left side of the road.

STEP 10 – Add a sensor

Select the **car sprite.**

Pick the **Rectangle** tool.

Choose red.

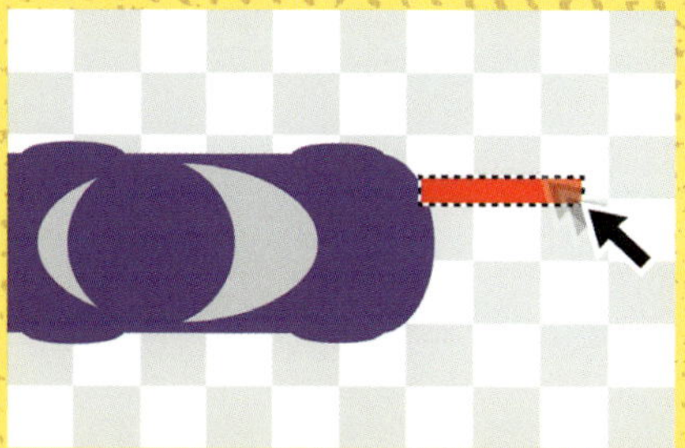

Drag out a long, thin rectangle to be the sensor beam. Make sure it looks like this.

If the car senses an object on its left, or the left side of the road, then it needs to move away from it by turning right.

STEP 11 – Turn right

Click the **Code** tab and change your code so it looks like this:

```
when [flag] clicked
set size to 20 %
forever
    move 2 steps
    if <color [red] is touching [white] ?> then
        turn ↻ 15 degrees
```

Set these colors by clicking inside the square, then clicking the Pipette and clicking on a color from the Stage.

Check if the red sensor beam is touching white (off the road).

If so, turn right 15 degrees.

Click the flag to test the code!

How it works:

1. To start, the loop keeps the car moving in a straight line.

2. When the sensor beam detects that the edge of the road is ahead...

3. ...the car starts to turn to the right.

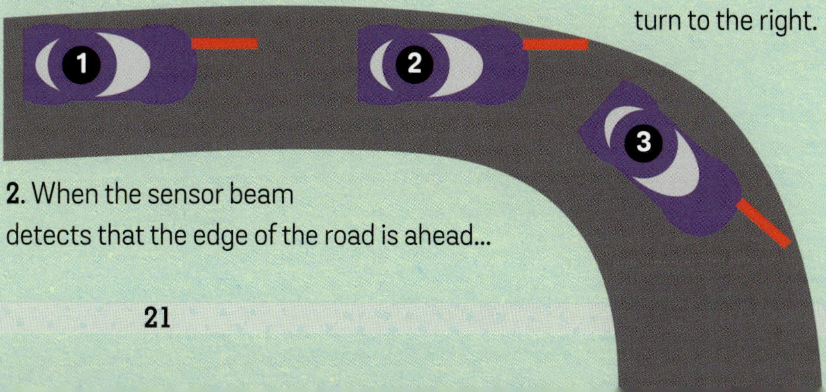

Real roads turn left and right. We're going to change our road and add another sensor.

STEP 12 – Curve test

Click the **Stage** icon.

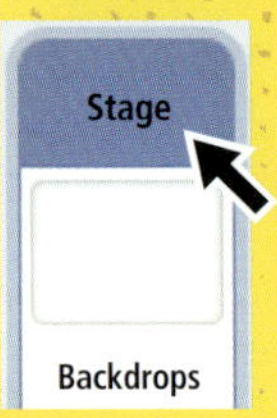

Choose the **Backdrops** tab.

Hover over the **Choose a Backdrop** button.

Click the **Brush** icon.

Click **Convert to Bitmap**.

Choose the **Brush** tool.

Pick dark gray.

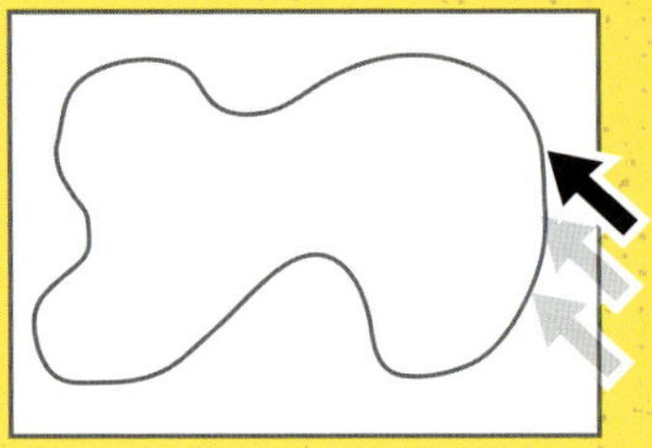

Draw a new road. Give it a lot of bends. Avoid tight corners.

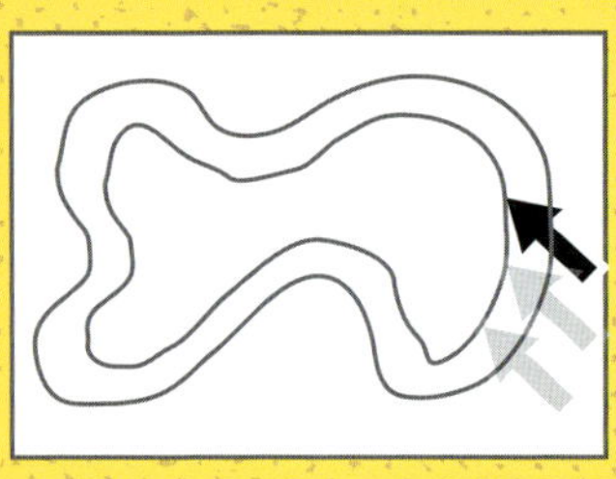

Now draw the inside of the road. Make sure there are no gaps.

Fill in between the two lines to make a thick gray road.

STEP 13 – Second sensor

Select the **car sprite**.

Pick the **Rectangle** tool.

Choose orange.

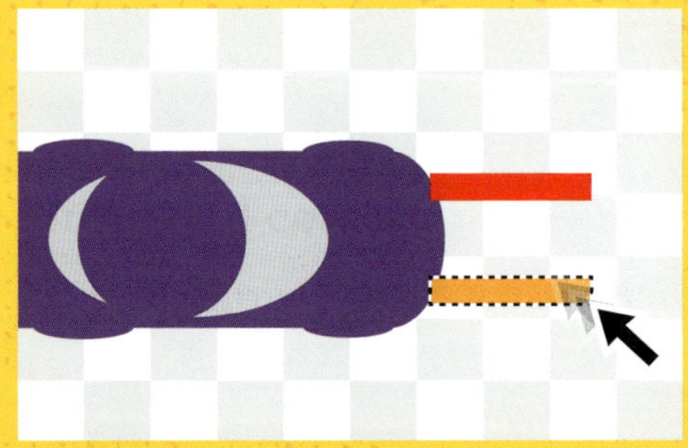

Draw an orange rectangle below the red one. This will be our second sensor beam.

STEP 14 – Code upgrade

We need to upgrade our code to include the new orange sensor beam. If it touches the edge of the road, the car needs to turn left.

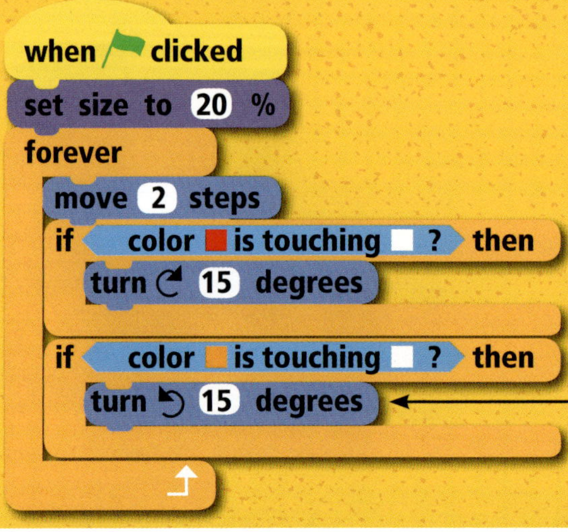

If the orange sensor beam is touching white, then run this code:

Turn left 15 degrees.

Test your code!

Investigate

What happens if you change the width and length of the red and orange sensor beams?

At the moment, the car turns 15 degrees when it detects an obstacle. Try changing this value. Does this make the car better or worse at driving?

Some self-driving cars only work at slow speeds. Our car moves 2 steps every time the loop runs. If we increase this value, does the car become dangerous? Experiment to find the fastest safe speed it can travel around your road.

Code challenge

Add a second car by duplicating the car sprite and its code. How about a third or fourth car?

Make each car travel at a different speed.

Add more code so the cars avoid each other. You might need to add another sensor to do this. It could make the cars stop, slow down, or reverse if they detect another car nearby.

Sensors

How do they work?

If you shout out "Hello" in the middle of an empty field, you won't hear anything. But try shouting inside a tunnel and you will hear an echo. This is caused by the sound bouncing back off the walls of the tunnel.

Real sensors and radar systems work in the same way. They send out a radio wave (radar) or an infrared beam of radiation (sensor). If there are any obstacles nearby, then part of the beam will bounce back.

If the object is close, then it will bounce back quickly. Sensors measure how long it takes the beam to bounce back, and use this value to calculate how far away the object is.

The Google self-driving car has no steering wheel, gas pedal, or brake. It does have sensors, but the car is a little more sophisticated than the one we coded. It uses cameras as well as sensors to find out where objects are.

The car uses *artificial intelligence* (AI) *software* to find out what the objects are. The software analyzes the size, speed, and the way the object moves. It then determines whether the object is another car, a bike, or a pedestrian, and what it should do.

Self-driving cars also use GPS technology to determine where they are—they don't want to get lost any more than human drivers do!

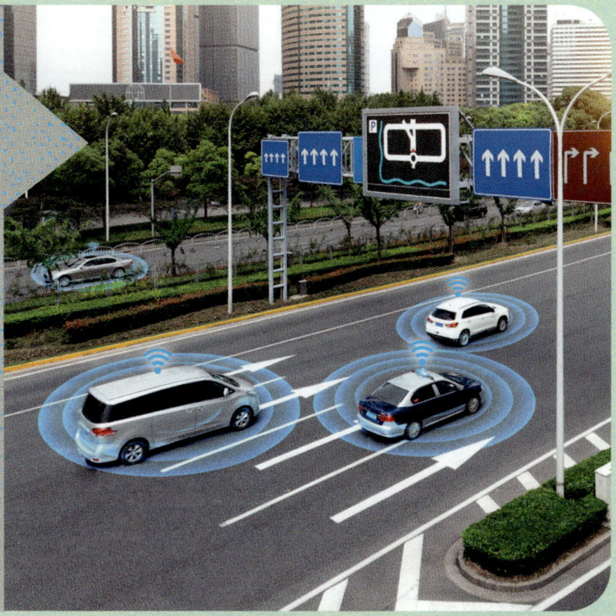

Hoverboard Scooters

Hoverboard scooters are a brand-new form of transportation made possible by new technology. The board doesn't actually hover, but a computer helps riders balance on just two wheels.

The rider moves and steers the hoverboard by leaning and pressing down on switches with their feet. Let's find out how they work by building our own with code.

STEP 1 – Remove the cat

Right-click the cat sprite and click **delete**.

STEP 2 – The background

Click the **Backdrops** tab.

For help, go to:
www.maxw.com

STEP 3 – Start drawing

Click **Convert to Bitmap**.

Choose the **Rectangle** tool.

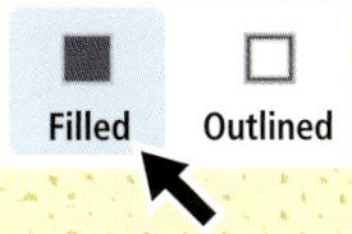

Pick **Filled**, then choose a color.

Draw a very large, pale blue rectangle for the sky.

Add a second brown rectangle for the ground.

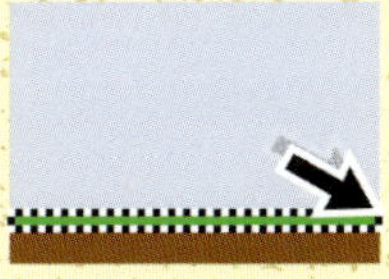

Draw a third thin, green rectangle to be the grass.

STEP 4 – Add a sprite

Hover over the **Choose a Sprite** button.

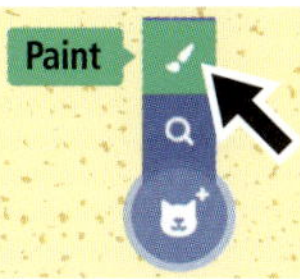

Click the **Brush** icon.

STEP 5 – We need wheels

Click **Convert to Bitmap.**

Now click the **Ellipse** tool.

Choose black.

Draw the tire in the center of the drawing area.

Add a gray wheel in the center of the tire.

STEP 6 – The rider

Select the **Rectangle** tool and choose a color.

Draw the rider's legs.

Then add their body.

Click the **Ellipse** tool, then pick a skin color.

Draw their head.

STEP 7 – Final details

Choose the **Line** tool and pick a color.

Make the line fairly thick.

Draw their arms.

Pick the **Brush** tool.

Add any final details.

STEP 8 – Start coding

We need a variable that can store the angle of the hoverboard.

Click the **Code** tab.

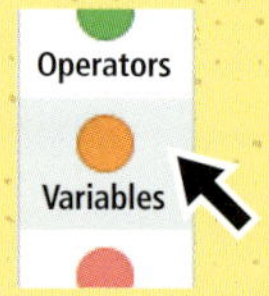

Click the **Variables** category.

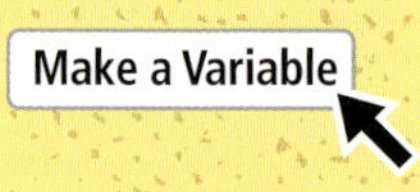

Click **Make a Variable**.

Type **angle**.

Click **OK**.

STEP 9 – The main code

Drag in this code.

```
when [green flag] clicked                        ← Run this code when the green flag is clicked:
point in direction (90)                          ← Make sure the hoverboard is upright.
go to x: (0)                                     ← Move it to the center of the Stage.
set size to (75) %                               ← Shrink it down to 75%.
say [Get ready!] for (2) secs                    ← Show a message.
repeat until <touching color [brown] ?>          ← Keep looping until the hoverboard hits the ground:
    set [angle] to (mouse x)                     ← Set the angle variable according to where the mouse is.
    change [angle] by (pick random (-2) to (2))  ← Change it slightly by a random amount.
    set [angle] to ((angle) / (2))               ← Divide the angle by 2.
    if <(angle) > (45)> then                     ← If the hoverboard is tipping over (more than 45 degrees):
        set [angle] to (100)                     ← Tip it right over (100 degrees).
    end
    if <(angle) < (-45)> then                    ← If it's tipping over backward (less than –45 degrees):
        set [angle] to (-100)                    ← Tip it right over (–100 degrees).
    end
    point in direction ((90) + (angle))          ← Position the hoverboard at the calculated angle that has been stored in the variable.
    change x by ((angle) / (5))                  ← Move the hoverboard left or right, according to how far over it is tipping.
end                                              ← Keep looping, unless the scooter rider has fallen over and hit the ground.
say [Ow!] for (2) secs                           ← Show a message.
```

Click the flag to test your code.

Here are some tips to help you put the code on page 26 together:

Setting the touching color code block:

`touching color ■`

First, click the color selector square.

Next, click the Pipette, then click on a color somewhere on the Stage.

Using random numbers:

`pick random -2 to 2`

Drag the **pick random** block into your code. Type in two numbers. The first one sets the smallest number you need, the second the largest. When the code runs, it will pick one for you.

Combining code blocks together:

`set angle to 0` — Start by dragging in a **set angle** block.

`set angle to ( / )` — Next, drag in a **division** block from the **Operators** group.

`set angle to (angle / )` — From the **Variables** group, drag in an **angle** block.

`set angle to (angle / 2)` — Type a 2 inside the **division** block.

Drag your scooter down so the wheels are touching the top of the grass. Use your mouse to balance your hoverboard. Move the mouse gently to the left or right of the screen to adjust your balance. Make sure your mouse pointer is in the middle of the screen when you start.

How it works

Steering
There is no steering wheel on a hoverboard. You steer by pushing or leaning farther on one foot. For example, pushing down harder on the right foot makes the motor on the right side go faster, turning the board to the left.

Wheels
There is a wheel on each side of the board.

Motors
Inside the board are two motors, one attached to each wheel.

Pivot
The hoverboard frame has two halves, which are joined in the middle by a pivot. This allows the rider to balance on each leg more easily.

Sensors
Special gyroscopes and sensors are used to measure how fast the wheels are turning and the angle of each half of the board.

Switches
The rider places each foot on a pedal. There are switches underneath the pedals. Leaning gently forward or backward activates the switches and tells the hoverboard to move.

Computer
An onboard computer reads data from the sensors and switches. It uses this information to decide how much power to send to each motor.

Hoverboard Game

Let's use our hoverboard scooter to make a catching game! Drive your scooter backward and forward to catch all the apples and score points.

STEP 1 – Before you start

Make sure you have all the code from the previous two pages in your computer and that your hoverboard works properly on-screen.

STEP 2 – Adding an apple

Click the **Choose a Sprite** button.

Choose the **Apple** sprite.

STEP 3 – The score

Make a variable that can store the score in the game.

Click the **Code** tab.

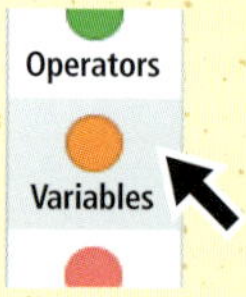

Click the **Variables** category.

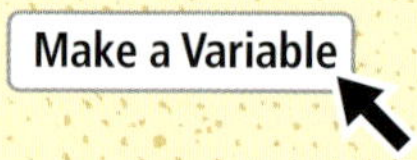

Click **Make a Variable.**

Type **score**.

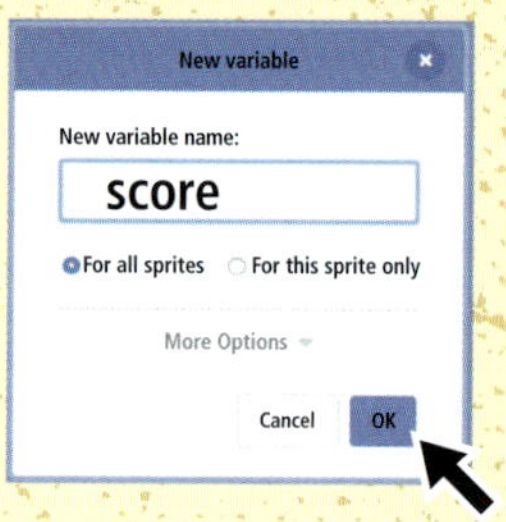

Click **OK**.

STEP 4 – Code the apple

Drag in this code to make the apple move:

```
when [flag] clicked                      ← Run this code when the green flag is clicked:
set size to (75) %                       ← Shrink the apple down to 75%.
set [score v] to (0)                     ← Reset the score to zero.
forever                                  ← Keep looping this code:
    go to [random position v]            ← Move the apple to a random place...
    set y to (160)                       ← ...but move it to the top of the screen.
    repeat until <touching color [ ] ?>  ← Keep looping until the apple hits the ground:
        change y by (-3)                 ← Move the apple downward.
        if <touching [Sprite1 v] ?> then ← If the apple has been caught by the hoverboard:
            start sound [pop v]          ← Play a sound effect.
            change [score v] by (1)      ← Increase the score.
            go to [random position v]    ← Go to a random place.
        end
    end
end
```

STEP 5 – More apples

Right-click the **apple**.

Click **duplicate**.

Duplicate the apple again, so you have three apples.

Click the flag to test your code.

Investigate

In the code for the hoverboard scooter, try adjusting the range of the random number that gets picked.

```
pick random (-5) to (5)
```

Code challenge

The hoverboard scooter falls over when the angle is more than 45 degrees or less than –45 degrees. Change the code to allow it to tip farther over before it falls.

Add a sound effect that is played when the scooter falls over.

Make the apples stop falling when they hit the scooter.

Bugs and Debugging

When you find your code isn't working as expected, stop and look through each command you have put in. Think about what you want it to do, and what it is really telling the computer to do. If you are entering one of the programs in this book, check that you have not missed a line. Some things to check:

Joining blocks properly:

✓
```
when flag clicked
repeat 10
    move 10 steps
```

✗
```
when flag clicked
repeat 10
move 10 steps
```

Select sprites before adding code:

Before you add code to a sprite, click on it in the **Sprites pane**. This will select it and make sure the code is assigned to it. If you don't do this, you may find your code is trying to control the wrong sprite!

X or Y?

```
set x to 0
set y to 0
```

y ↑ → x Don't mix them up!

The right size

A sprite that is the wrong size may stop your code from working. Change the set size percent value to make them fit properly.

Right color, wrong code?

```
set score to 1
change score by 1
```

Be precise. Many code blocks look very similar, but do completely different things!

Position variables and values carefully:

`change y by e` ✗

Don't type in variable names.

`change y speed` ✗

Don't just drop them on top of blocks.

`speed`

Drag them until a glowing white circle appears.

`change y by speed`

The value block will then snap into place.

Tips to reduce *bugs*:

- When things are working properly, spend time looking through your code so you understand each line.

Experiment and change your code. Try out different values.

To be good at *debugging*, you need to understand what each code block does and how your code works.

- Practice debugging! Make a very short program and get a friend to change one block only, while you aren't looking. Can you fix it?
- If you are making your own program, spend time drawing a diagram and planning it before you start. Try changing values if things don't work, and don't be afraid to start again—you will learn from it.

Glossary

algorithm Rules or steps followed to make something work or complete a task

artificial intelligence (AI) Software that does more than just follow steps. AI systems respond with apparent intelligence to outside events.

bug An error in a program that stops it from working properly

code block A draggable instruction icon used in Scratch

debug To remove bugs (or errors) from a program

degrees The units used to measure angles

Global Positioning System (GPS) A way of finding out exactly where something is by measuring signals from satellites orbiting Earth

gyroscope (gyro) A device that detects the angle it is positioned at and sends this information to a computer

icon A small, clickable image on a computer

loop Repeating one or more commands a number of times

random A number that can't be predicted

right-click To click the right mouse button

sensor A device that measures something in the real world, such as how far away an object is, and sends the answer to a computer as a value

software A computer program containing instructions written in code

sprite An object with a picture on it that moves around the stage

stage The place in Scratch that sprites move around

steps Small movements made by sprites

system A combination of software, hardware, sensors, and information

variable Part of a program that stores a value that can change

Index and Further Information

FURTHER INFORMATION

Gifford, Clive. *Awesome Algorithms and Creative Coding*. Crabtree Publishing Company, 2015.

Wainewright, Max. *How to Code: A Step-By-Step Guide to Computer Coding*. Sterling Children's Books, 2016.

Wainewright, Max. *I'm a Scratch Coder.* Crabtree Publishing Company, 2018.

CAPERCAILLIES

MAP AND TRACK

Capercaillies are a type of grouse that live in large **boreal** forests that have many sources of food, such as bilberries. Bilberries are some of the most common plants growing in the Vosges. At one time, the Vosges provided the perfect habitat for capercaillies. Today, because so many trees have been cut down, there is less food and shelter for them. Now, there are only about 100 capercaillies in the Vosges Mountains. A program to protect them is in place to help keep them from disappearing completely.

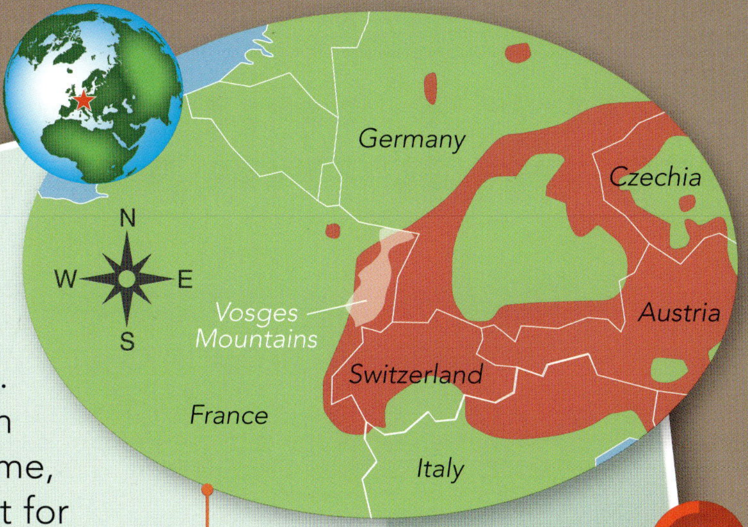

This map shows the range of the capercaillies in the Vosges Mountains and surrounding areas.

Key
Capercaillie range

Capercaillies mainly eat conifer needles in winter. In the spring and summer, they also eat buds, flowers, leaves, and shrubs.

Black Hills

The Black Hills spread across the Great Plains through parts of South Dakota and Wyoming. These mountains began to form 600 billion years ago. The Black Hills have four ecosystems: the Rocky Mountains, the Great Plains, **deciduous** forest, and boreal forest.

Great horned owls are large birds of prey that have few natural predators.

Hunting

The Black Hills get their name from the ponderosa pine trees that make the hills look black from a distance. Mule deer and white-tailed deer are common animals here. They grow thick fur coats in the winter to keep warm. Mountain lions track deer by following their footprints in the snow. The lions' big paws help them run through the snow quickly to chase their prey. Great horned owls hunt mainly for rabbits, hares, and mice. Their soft feathers help them fly quietly so they can sneak up on their prey.

Red-bellied snakes hide under rocks, leaves, and logs in mountain meadows and woodlands.

Sneaky Snakes

Red-bellied snakes search for a place to hibernate in winter. They often take shelter in abandoned anthills. They stay together in groups that may even include other snake **species**. Red-bellied snakes often feed on slugs and snails. Their long, blade-like teeth are adapted for eating slugs and pulling snails out of their shells.

STOP AND SPOT

FRINGE-TAILED MYOTIS

The fringe-tailed myotis is a small bat with reddish to dark-brown fur. This bat is at risk due to habitat loss and the poisonous chemicals used in farming in areas where it lives. The **rare** bat is found in mountainous areas in southwestern Canada, the western United States, and Mexico. It is known to live in caves in the southern Black Hills. The fringe-tailed myotis eats up to half its weight in insects each night. It plays a key role in the ecosystem by helping to control insect populations. It hibernates throughout the winter.

The fringe-tailed myotis is most active from April through September.

The Black Hills get their name from the Lakota words Paha sapa, which mean "hills that are black."

Hawaiian-Emperor Chain

The Hawaiian-Emperor Chain is the largest volcano chain on Earth. It stretches from the island of Hawaii in the southeast to Kure **Atoll** in the northwest. It consists of a mostly undersea mountain range. Only a few rise above the surface of the ocean to make up 132 islands, **reefs**, and atolls.

This extinct volcano, part of the Hawaiian-Emperor Chain, towers over the surrounding plains.

Adaptive Plants

Many of Hawaii's plants, such as pineapples and orchids, were brought to the islands by visitors. Some plants have adapted to life on Hawaii. For example, in other parts of the world, mint has strong-tasting leaves that help keep predators away. In Hawaii, the plant is not threatened by anything, so a tasteless form of mint grows there. The same is true for nettles. Usually, these plants have stinging hairs on their leaves. In Hawaii, the leaves do not sting because the plants have no predators.

Nettles are used by insects to lay their eggs and provide food for their young.

Predator Caterpillars

Carnivorous caterpillars perch on leaves and stems waiting to catch their insect prey. They eat flies, moths, crickets, cockroaches, and even other caterpillars. They snatch their prey with their strong, sharp claws. In other parts of the world, this same species feeds only on plants. No one knows why they have adapted to eating insects in Hawaii.

HAWKSBILL TURTLES

MAP AND TRACK

Hawksbill turtles live all over the world in places that have a **tropical** climate. They get their name from their hooked beak, which looks similar to a hawk's beak. Each year, females come ashore to lay their eggs on nesting sites on the Hawaiian Islands. Hawksbills are endangered, mainly due to human activities. Some people kill them for their shells, or to eat their eggs or flesh. Turtles die when they get caught in fishing nets.

This map shows the nesting areas of the hawksbill turtle.

Key
Hawksbill turtle nesting area

Hawksbills mainly eat sea sponges and use their beak to dig for prey among corals and rocks.

Baby hawksbill turtles race toward the sea when they hatch from eggs laid in the sand.

Virunga Chain

The volcanic Virunga Mountains stretch along the borders of Rwanda, Democratic Republic of the Congo, and Uganda in East Africa. The Virunga range is known for its many different ecosystems that vary from lakes and **marshes** to **peat bogs**, forests, and glaciers.

Mountain gorillas are shy, gentle animals.

Park Place

Virunga National Park is the most **biodiverse** park in all of Africa. This is due to its different elevations, heavy rainfall, and rich soil. Bamboo is one of the most common plants in Virunga. It grows high in the mountains and can survive long periods of cold, harsh weather. Many animals, such as mountain gorillas and golden monkeys, need bamboo as part of their diet.

MOUNTAIN GORILLAS

MAP AND TRACK

About one-third of the world's mountain gorillas live in the forests of Virunga National Park. Mountain gorillas have long, thick fur that helps keep them warm in the cold mountains. The damp forests there have lots of herbs and other plants for them to eat. Only about 1,000 mountain gorillas remain in the world. Their biggest threat is humans. Many mountain gorillas have been poached. Some have been killed in **civil wars**. Others have been caught in traps meant for antelopes. Some catch human diseases and die. Trained rangers help protect Virunga National Park from human threats.

This map shows the range of the mountain gorilla in the Virunga Mountains.

Mountain Monkey

One of the most endangered animals in the Virunga range is the golden monkey. Humans are their main threat. Some people hunt them. Others cut down the bamboo the monkeys need to live. Golden monkeys are found only in Central Africa. The climate varies in their natural habitat, so these monkeys can change their diet from season to season. They eat mainly fruits in the dry season, and bamboo and plant buds in the wet season.

Golden monkeys spend most of the day at the top of bamboo trees.

A Small Comeback

Virunga was once home to the largest hippo population in Africa. Their numbers have dropped from nearly 30,000 in the 1970s to fewer than 1,000 today. Many have been killed in local wars. Others are poached for their teeth and meat. Their numbers are growing again due to protection programs.

Hippo eyes, ears, and nostrils are high on their heads, so they can see, hear, and breathe while their bodies are underwater.

Catskills

The Catskills are part of the Appalachian Mountains, which stretch from Newfoundland and Labrador in Canada, to Alabama in the United States. Located in southeastern New York State, the Catskills are not like any other mountains. They formed when rivers and streams made deep valleys to create mountain-like cliffs.

Young deer are called fawns and have a reddish-brown coat with white spots. This helps camouflage them in long grass.

Run and Hide

White-tailed deer are the most common large mammals found in the Catskills. Their main predators are coyotes, cougars, and humans, but the deer have strong legs for running away from predators. They can reach speeds of up to 30 miles per hour (48 kph) and jump up to 10 feet (3 m) high. They grow thick underfur and long hairs in winter to keep them warm. They also store fat under their skin to keep them warm, and to give them extra energy in winter when there is little food to eat.

Wonderful Rodents

Beavers have webbed feet and a large flat tail to help them move swiftly through the rivers that run through the Catskills. They have a thick undercoat to keep them warm in the freezing mountain temperatures and icy water. Long, dark **guard hairs** keep water from soaking into the beavers' fur. They also act as a form of insulation.

Beavers produce a type of oil that they rub all over their bodies to waterproof their fur.

BOBCATS

Bobcats are wild cats that live lower down the Catskill Mountains. These cats get their name from their short tail, which looks like it has been cut off, or bobbed. Their fur changes color with the seasons to help them blend in with their surroundings. In New York State, bobcat numbers are on the rise, so they are often trapped or hunted for their fur to help control their population. However, the government closely tracks the number of bobcats that are hunted each year to make sure they continue to **thrive**.

This is how the bobcat population is hunted in the Catskills and the surrounding area of New York State.

Key
Bobcat hunting allowed
No bobcat hunting allowed

Bobcats have excellent hearing. They can turn their ears in different directions to pick up sounds all around them.

Eastern coyotes in the Catskill Mountains are larger than other coyotes in other parts of the country, so they are often mistaken for wolves.

North Island Volcanic Plateau

Bubbling mud pools, rocky terraces, massive caves, steaming hot springs, and shooting **geysers** are all part of the North Island Volcanic **Plateau** in New Zealand. Over time, layers of ash and rocks poured out from volcanoes to form a plateau that rises high above sea level.

Geckos have flexible tails that can grip surfaces like a fifth limb.

Lots of Lizards

The Volcanic Plateau is home to many types of lizards, such as forest geckos and Wellington green geckos. Geckos are well adapted for living in cold environments. When it is freezing cold, they will find a safe place to rest until the temperature warms. When the weather is very cold, geckos will move farther down the mountain, below the frost line. They may stay in rock crevices and the burrows of other animals to keep warm. Some geckos store fat in their tails to use when food is scarce or while they hibernate.

*The blue duck's beak works like a **sieve** to filter out insects and **larvae** from the water.*

Bountiful Birds

Kiwis are flightless birds found in the Volcanic Plateau. They hunt at night when they are less likely to be seen by predators. Kiwis do not see well. They have hairs at the base of their beak that help them avoid running into things at night. Blue ducks are one of the most endangered species in New Zealand. Habitat loss and human activities are threats to these ducks. They are also at risk from predators that have been introduced to the habitat such as stoats, a **non-native** species.

BROWN MUDFISH

Brown mudfish are a type of freshwater fish that are native to New Zealand. They live in swamps and wetlands. In the summer, the water there dries up, and mudfish burrow into wet mud to keep their bodies moist. They go into a sleep-like state, until the water returns in the fall when they quickly lay their eggs. This gives their young the longest time possible to grow before the water dries up again.

This map shows the distribution of brown mudfish in New Zealand.

Brown mudfish are at risk due to the loss of wetlands from human development.

Kiwis have nostrils at the ends of their long beaks to help them sniff out food from inside rotten logs or sense it under the ground.

Mountains in Danger

Mountains provide habitats for countless plant and animal species. They also store snow and ice that feed rivers and streams all year round. All of the planet's major rivers start in mountains. But mountains are at risk from being damaged by human activity.

Human activities such as logging (top) and pollution (bottom) are two of the threats to mountain biomes.

Future Thinking

Logging, mining, farming, tourism, and building are just a few of the many threats to mountains. They cause mountain forests to be cut down and nearby water to be polluted with **waste**. Plants can no longer live there, and animals are forced to move elsewhere for food and shelter. One way to save mountains from further damage is to create special areas that have laws about hunting and building.

Climate Change

Many mountain glaciers are melting due to global warming. This could lead to **droughts**, landslides, and floods. It could cause drinking water shortages around the world. Rising sea levels could destroy cities and towns along the coastline. Humans contribute to climate change by burning coal and oil. Using renewable energy sources, such as water, wind, and **solar** power, can help prevent climate change. People can cut back on their use of coal and oil by riding their bikes or walking to school or work, using energy-saving **appliances**, and recycling or reducing the amount of waste they produce.

MAP AND TRACK IT!

Now it is your turn. You can create a map to track endangered mountain animals. Here is what you need to do:

1. Choose one of the mountain ranges in this book.
2. Create a map to show the mountain range (see page 6 for help).
3. Research the animals that live in the mountains you have chosen. Which ones are endangered? Choose two or three endangered animals to track.
4. Color in the map to show where they are found. See the box below to learn how to find map references for your chosen animals.
5. Make a key to show what the different colors mean.

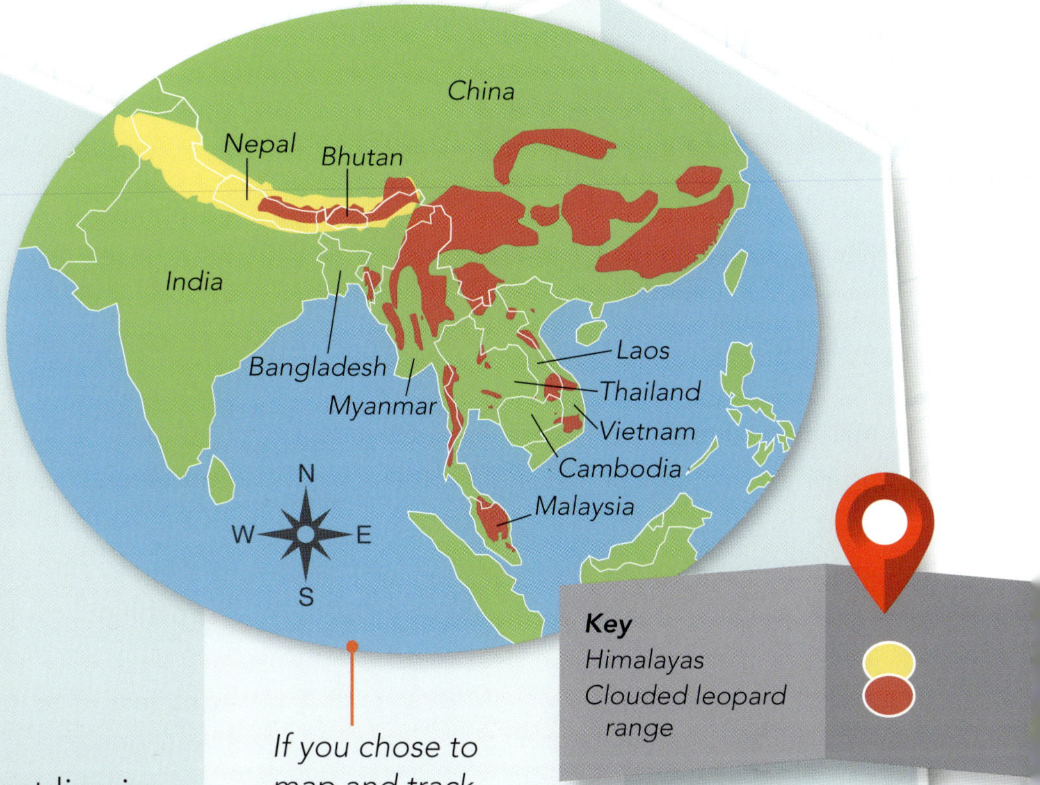

If you chose to map and track the clouded leopard, your map would look like this.

THE IUCN

The International Union for Conservation of Nature (IUCN) is a great resource for your map. The IUCN is an international group of scientists that track animals and decide whether they are endangered. They produce reports on many different species, including maps to show where they currently live. The website for their "Red List," where you can search by species, is on page 31.

Glossary

Please note: Some **bold-faced** words are defined where they appear in the text.

adapted Changed over time to better suit an environment

altitude Height above ground or sea level

amphibians Cold-blooded animals that can live on land and in the water

appliances Pieces of equipment, such as blenders, that are powered by electricity and that are used for a specific purpose

atoll A ring-shaped reef, island, or chain of islands made of coral

biodiverse Having a large variety of plants and animals in a certain place

biomes Large geographical areas with the same general landscape, climate, and life

border An imaginary line that separates two countries or regions

boreal Relating to cold and snowy regions

breed To produce young

broad-leaved Wide, flat leaves

camouflage To blend in with the natural environment

carnivorous Eats mainly meat

civil wars Conflicts between people who live in the same place

classified Arranged in a certain order

climate Weather patterns in a region

cones The woody fruit of a conifer tree where the seeds are stored

conifers Evergreen shrubs and trees that have needlelike or scalelike leaves

conservation groups Organizations that work to protect nature

deciduous Describing a tree that sheds its leaves once a year

diameter A line that passes through the center of a circle from one side to the other

droughts Long periods of time with no rain

ecosystem All the living and nonliving things in a certain area

endangered When a species is in danger of dying out completely

filter To remove solids from liquids

foothills Low hills at the bottom of a mountain or a range of mountains

geysers Jets of hot water from under the ground that usually shoot into the air

glacial lakes Lakes formed from melting glaciers

guard hairs Long, coarse hairs that protect the fur underneath

habitat The natural environment

heatstroke Illness caused when the body overheats

hibernate To spend the winter sleeping

highlands Hilly, mountainous regions

illegal Against the law

insulation Material that keeps heat from escaping

larvae Young insects

mammals Warm-blooded animals that produce milk to feed their young

marshes Areas that are always waterlogged

mate To pair up to produce young

non-native Not originally found in a specific place

peat bogs Wetland areas of a thick, black, mud-like substance called peat

pesticides Chemicals used on crops to kill insects that damage the plants

plateau An area of flat, high ground

poaching Hunting or killing illegally

predators Animals that kill and eat other animals

prey Animals that are hunted and killed by other animals for food

reefs A ridge of coral, rock, or sand just above or below the sea surface

reptiles Cold-blooded animals that have scales on their bodies and usually lay eggs

salt flats Areas of flat land covered with salt

sieve A utensil that separates solids from liquids

solar To do with the Sun

species A specific class of plants or animals

tectonic plates Massive pieces of Earth's outer layer

thermal springs Naturally hot water that comes up from under the ground

thrive To grow strong

torpor A state of inactivity

toxins Substances that are poisonous

tropical Having a hot and wet climate

waste Garbage or chemicals

Learning More

Books

Bow, James. *Mountains Inside Out* (Ecosystems Inside Out). Crabtree Publishing Company, 2015.

Kalman, Bobbie. *Where on Earth are Mountains?* (Explore the Continents). Crabtree Publishing Company, 2014.

London, Martha. *Mountains* (Landforms). Focus Readers, 2018.

Spilsbury, Richard. *At Home in the Mountains* (Home in the Biome). PowerKids Press, 2016.

Websites

www.iucnredlist.org
Explore the IUCN's Red List of animals that are threatened, endangered, or nearly extinct.

www.mountain.org
Learn about conservation efforts at mountain ranges around the world.

www.nationalgeographic.com/science/earth/surface-of-the-earth/mountains
Discover different types of mountains and how they form.

Index

ABOUT THE AUTHOR

Heather C. Hudak has written hundreds of books for children and edited thousands more. When she is not writing, she enjoys traveling all over the world. Heather has been to more than 50 countries. She has roamed the African savanna in Kenya, hiked the Rocky Mountains in Canada, sailed across the Atlantic Ocean, and explored the rain forests of Costa Rica.